Bey___ __at Gilded
Euphoria

Nicky Saje

BookLeaf
Publishing

Beyond That Gilded Euphoria © 2023 Nicky
Saje

All rights reserved.

No part of this publication may be
reproduced, stored in a retrieval system, or
transmitted, in any form or by any means,
electronic, mechanical, photocopying,
recording, or otherwise, without the prior
written permission of the presenters.

Nicky Saje asserts the moral right to be
identified as the author of this work.

Presentation by *BookLeaf Publishing*

Web: www.bookleafpub.com

E-mail: info@bookleafpub.com

ISBN: 9789395969109

First edition 2023

Dedicated to my inner child. We're still here, alive and fighting.

You made it, kid.

ACKNOWLEDGEMENT

Thank you to everybody that has stuck by me over the years. You know who you are. And thank you to all the new people in my life, you guys rock. A big thank you to my family for being my biggest support system and always picking me up when I fail. Another big thank you to my best friend for believing in me every single day and being my constant rock during the bad days.

All of you have inspired me and supported me throughout my rollercoaster of a journey. I seriously wouldn't still be here if it wasn't for you guys. It was a rough few years there, and I don't blame anybody for leaving, to those who did. This book is also dedicated to my past friends and lovers. Again, you know who you are. All of you significantly impacted me in ways that I will never forget. I learned hard lessons that I will carry with me for the rest of my life. I haven't forgotten about any of you, and I wish you all the very best.

I would also like to thank myself. During those times of darkened isolation, all I had was myself to turn to. I'm the one who decided that I didn't want to stay stuck where I was. I'm the one who decided to stay alive. I'm the one who decided to get help. I'm the one that made the change. And the 'me' of yesterday is so proud of the 'me' of today. We aren't there yet, but we're so much closer to our ideal selves than we were a year ago.

Also, thanks to my future readers and fans. I hope to be a safe space for you all.

PREFACE

I have never been shy about sharing my story or my struggles.

I've always been an open book. An 'over-sharer', as some may call it. I am not afraid to take to social media to outline my struggles with mental health and gender-identity. The reasoning for this is simple: I want to use my unapologetic voice to make people feel less alone. If one person reads my post and relates to it, I want them to know that I am a safe space for them to come talk to. Over the years of being open about my shadows, I've had so many people privately reach out to me about their own demons that they struggle with. This is my goal. If I can be that safe space for somebody who feels like they can't turn to anyone else, then my mission is fulfilled.

Most of my life was spent hating the fact that I am an empath. I hated feeling other people's emotions. It was draining and exhausting. I used to isolate myself and became an introverted hermit for several years - afraid of the world and the entanglement of feelings that hide within its inhabitants.

Now, at 25 years old, I have grown to be grateful for this trait. It helps me become a better writer. It allows me to dive into complex characters and completely submerge myself in their personality and distinct way of thinking. It also allows me to understand multiple points of view on a topic, even if I don't agree with the morality of the beliefs.

One of my favorite words that I've ever come across is 'sonder'. It is, in as simple terms as possible, the abstract and profound realization that every person in the entire world has their own life and their own struggles and own unique processes of thinking. The term also nods towards the collective ignorance to this fact. People don't all realize this fact, especially today. Everyone is so wrapped up in their own world and their own demons that they sometimes forget that other people are their own protagonists of a story too. In your story, you may see yourself as a victim. In another person's story, you may be the villain.

Perspective is so important. And in my writing, I aim to challenge and manipulate people's perspectives on difficult, controversial topics. This is why I write what I write. It is my life mission to create some sort of empathetic discomfort while people read my work, especially if it is towards something that they've never experienced. Or, as previously stated, to let people with similar struggles know that they are not alone.

I write about what I am experiencing. I intertwine my personal life with my art. Over the years, my writing has dramatically changed depending on how old I am and what I am experiencing at that point in my life.

Nicky Saje
He/him/his

Apricity Among the Ash

The fire took everything from me.
The flames spawned from my own lips.
Raging around, burning everything in sight.
As I crawl and stumble out of the smoldering
wreckage,
I squint up towards the sky.
The blinding rays kiss my charred cheeks,
Reminding me of a new day.
The fire took everything from me,
And yet, gave me everything in return.
Like a phoenix reborn,
I have finally found my
Apricity among the ash.

Among the Ash, We Thrive

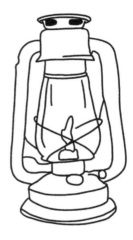

Dancing around, high off of chaos' kiss.
The smoldering sky rains ash upon my skin.
In the aftermath of the eruption,
I stumble around the charred remains.
A maniacal laugh bubbles up in my throat.
Is this freedom? Or is this hell?
This never-ending cycle of burning everything
down and
Crawling back up to enlightened insanity.
I grab your hand and lead the way down the
simmering path,
Throwing my head back with a wild grin.
For even though this looks like a devastating
disaster,
Among the ash, we thrive.

My Pick-Pocket Personalities

I am addicted to trying people on.
Not in a literal sense,
Or even a sexual sense.
No.
It runs so much deeper than just physical.
It is a skill that those teetering on the
Borderline
Of psychosis and reality
Have mastered.
For instance,
I'm great at beginnings.
I can play the part
And mirror people's thoughts and ideals
Perfectly
And seem like the perfect new companion or
lover.

That's not the problem.
The problem is that
It doesn't last.
My pick-pocket personalities fade away.
My mind grows tired
Playing pretend.
It is exhausting.

I do not want to play this game anymore.
For I feel like I never truly gain a sense of
My true self.
My mind is a patchwork quilt of all the people
I have ever met
And been close to,
Being haphazardly held together by
Crooked, bloodied staples.

Am I me?
Or am I them?

Can I ever be me?

An Abrupt Pause

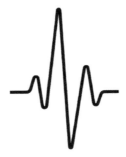

I ended my life the same as I began it.

Scrambling to feel the rays of the blinding sun.
I clawed at the sky,
My throat outstretched
As I desperately shouted words of prayer.
I begged for relief, for an end
To this enlightened insanity
That is being.
Pleaded with whatever higher power is out there
To salvage what was left of my soul.
To let me rest.
I was tired.
There was no light at the end of the tunnel for
me.
I had been searching for years with no luck.
Just an entangled maze of dark tunnels and
dungeons

Below an elaborate collapsing foundation.
This is it. This is peace.

Except,
My life didn't end there.
It was more of an abrupt pause
Then an actual stop.

I was still here.

The Game

Don't play the game with me.

The game of who can care less.
Because I will win.

I can turn it off with ease.
Feel everything and then nothing all at once.
I can stare blankly into your eyes
And tell you I hate you
And mean it
When I loved you a few seconds prior.

Splitting is a dark art.
All or nothing.
Black or white.
Hot or cold.
I love you, I hate you.

How can you know who you are?
When you're constantly flipping back and forth
Between one extreme to another.
How can you know who you are?

Beyond That Gilded Euphoria

Everyone has something
That they desire.
A person, a place, money, a type of food.
Everybody has something that makes them
Question themselves.
Something that makes them
Do things
That sometimes contradict their morals
And core beliefs.

I crave a feeling.
The feeling of being normal.
That 'aha!' moment of how life is supposed to
feel.
The moment when I have finally found what I

Have been searching for my entire life.
I crave the euphoric yet ignorant insanity that
comes
With being alive
And care-free.

I had that moment during a cool summer
evening
The first time that I tried crystal meth.
I slept with the man with long hair
Not because I desired him-
No,
I desired what he was going to give me.

I was awake for four days,
Choking on the feeling of completeness.
This is what I had been missing.
I was finally capable of becoming
The best version of myself.
My ideal self.

I was in control, I told myself
As I snorted several lines first thing each
morning.
I've always been in control.
I've never gotten addicted to anything else.
Weed, alcohol, coke, pills...
None had an addictive effect on me.
This won't be any different, I told myself

As I started injecting the crushed up crystals into
my veins
Because snorting wasn't enough anymore.

I didn't realize that I couldn't stop until I tried
to.
It was only four days,
But it felt like an eternity

Of unimaginable suffering.
With only one way to stop it.

As I spiraled downward into a dark abyss
With collapsed, bruised veins
And numb thoughts,
I surrendered to the looming chaos.
I suffocated on the loss of control,
The total dependence on this dangerous poison
Overtaking my every waking thought.

It became the one thing in the world that I truly
desired,
Because it brought me that feeling
Of enjoyment of life.
It reminded me
Of why I was alive.
It flooded me with radical innocence,
And childlike wonder and joy.
I was superhuman.
I could do anything.

But it was all fake.
It was slowly poisoning me.
Masking the issues instead of dealing with them.
Pushing them to the side, letting them build up
To explode later on.
I knew I had to bring a stop to the gilded
euphoria
Before it killed me.

Dialectic of Sobriety

Two things happened when I got clean.

I was a slave to my sobriety.
And yet,

I was finally free.

The Lonely Masochist

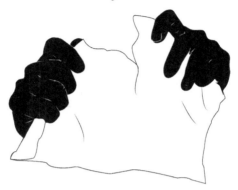

When I was a child,
I would pick at my crusted scabs
Until they bled.
My teachers would yell at me to stop.
But I liked the pain.

When I was a teenager,
I would use a broken razor to slit my wrists
Until they bled.
My parents and friends pleaded with me to stop.
But I liked the pain.

When I was a young adult,
I would use a needle to tear holes into my flesh
Until they bled.

Nobody pleaded for me to stop,
Because I didn't tell anybody.

I knew that I had to be the one
To tell myself to stop this time,
But I liked the pain.

A Soldier's Last Battle

I choke out a prayer, despite my hesitant disdain.
I forcefully crane my neck to the side.
I'm lying in the dirt next to a poor, wounded soul
that is seeping out crimson pain
Onto the blood-stained grass, knowing that I
have to hide
From the demons lurking around,
Creeping in the darkness, searching for a
weakened victim.
My hand covers my mouth, muffling the sound
Escaping my chapped lips. My rapture lies
within
A cracked sarcophagus, far from light.
I can no longer hold back my woeful war cry
For I know that this is my final fight.
And that every soldier must one day die.

The City Built Into A Mountain

In a city
Built onto the side of a mountain
Carved from pain and death,
I find myself wondering.

In a city
With crumbling, decaying buildings
And a flooding new community of starving
artists,
I find myself wondering.

Wondering if this
Gilded gentrification
Is a good thing;
Rewriting the name of the city
Spinning it into a positive, aesthetic light.

Or wondering if this
Gilded gentrification
is a bag thing;

Erasing the horrors
That were bestowed upon the original
inhabitants.
Their souls forever stuck here,
And their houses of suffering
Are now entertaining stops on popular Ghost
Tours.

My Decalcomania

I used to live in a demented, misshaped
decalcomania.
Both sides
Never quite matching.

On one hand,
Picture perfect.
Misleading social media posts.
Following the trends.
The perfect child.
With big hopes and dreams to follow.
My porcelain doppelgänger.

On the other hand,
Drowning in the bottomless abyss.
Poison in my veins,
Scars on my wrists.
Angry and choking on the loneliness.
Begging to be understood.
My tattered rag doll

Being dragged around by a withered arm.

My demented decalcomania.
Never quite matching.

Yet, never wanting the two sides
To fully match.

But I've stopped the disconnect.
A transparent awakening
Of the soul.
The thick fog disappears.

My decalcomania,
Although not exact,
is now closer to a perfect mirror image
Of either side.

Antibodies for Each Other

Taking turns being wrong.
One of us is never right.
Replaying a broken record's jumbled song.
Neither of us can give up the fight.

Worshiping the physical body,
But hesitant to accept the mind.
A mismatched pair filled with antibodies
For each other's lives.

Two Sides of a Sunset

One side was red.
An infuriating rage burning behind a cracked rib
cage,
Desperately clawing to be released.
The color of blood,
and the beginning of sunsets.

The other was purple.
A deep abyss of emotion and tenderness,
Silently sobbing to be understood.
The color of jewels,
And the end of sunsets.

Together, they were orange.
An explosion of forbidden vibrancy,
Dancing along the charred volcanic ash.
I was two sides of a sunset,
Entangled together by golden hues of chaos.

My Gordian Knot

Tying knots in my thoughts.
My twisted mental Shibari,
Suspended above an
Entangled foundation
Rising above
A decaying terrain.

Upon My Liar's Chair

I sit
Upon my liar's chair.
An iron throne of deceit,
With a crown of thorns.
The blood from my scalp
Streaks down
And mixes with my tears.
I cry.
For all I ever wanted was to be alone.
Away from it all.
Everything and everyone.
Yet I am doomed to chronically crave intimacy
While I sit by myself in my castle of uncharted
sins.

Can't You See Me?

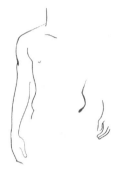

Can't you see me?

You can see my eyes.
And my lips
Upon my pale, freckled face.
But can't you see me?
For who I am?
For who I want to be?
For who I am meant to be?

Can't you see me
As the person I should've been born?

Better to Speak

Somewhere in Northern Italy,
I sit perched upon the grassy bank of my local
lake.
Apricot in hand,
A copy of "Heptameron" by Marguerite de
Navarre in the other.
"Is it better to speak or to die?"
I ask myself.
I ponder these words
As they pertain to my life.
Better to speak, I say.
Yet, cursed with the grueling anxieties of myself.
Wanting to speak up,
Yet doomed to die quietly.

*Inspired by Andre Aciman's *Call Me By Your Name*

You Love Being Loved.

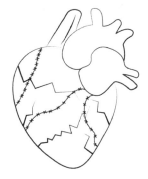

And here we are again
Another lost friendship
Like counting belt loops.
Confessions of unrequited love
Met with my compacted frustrations.
"Why does this always happen
To me?"
I ask.
"Because you love being loved,"
My friend replies.

Furiously Trudging Forward
Out of Spite

Another swinging low point.
Daunting yet not meaningless-
These lessons.
And yet, here comes the upswing.
Rising my sword high
With a tattered war cry.
Furiously trudging forward
Out of pure spite.

Fires In My Forest

The dancing embers light up my eyes
As you stand on the treeline
And twirl around in joyful glee.
I stand next to you.
Screaming.
For you set fires to my forest,
Because you wanted to watch me burn.

Printed in the USA
CPSIA information can be obtained
at www.ICGtesting.com
LVHW021459261024
794889LV00002B/97

9 789395 969109